I0509456

This Coloring Book Belongs to:

DINOSAUR COLLECTION

STEGOSAURUS

TYRANNOSAURUS

TRICERATOPS

BRACHIOSAURUS

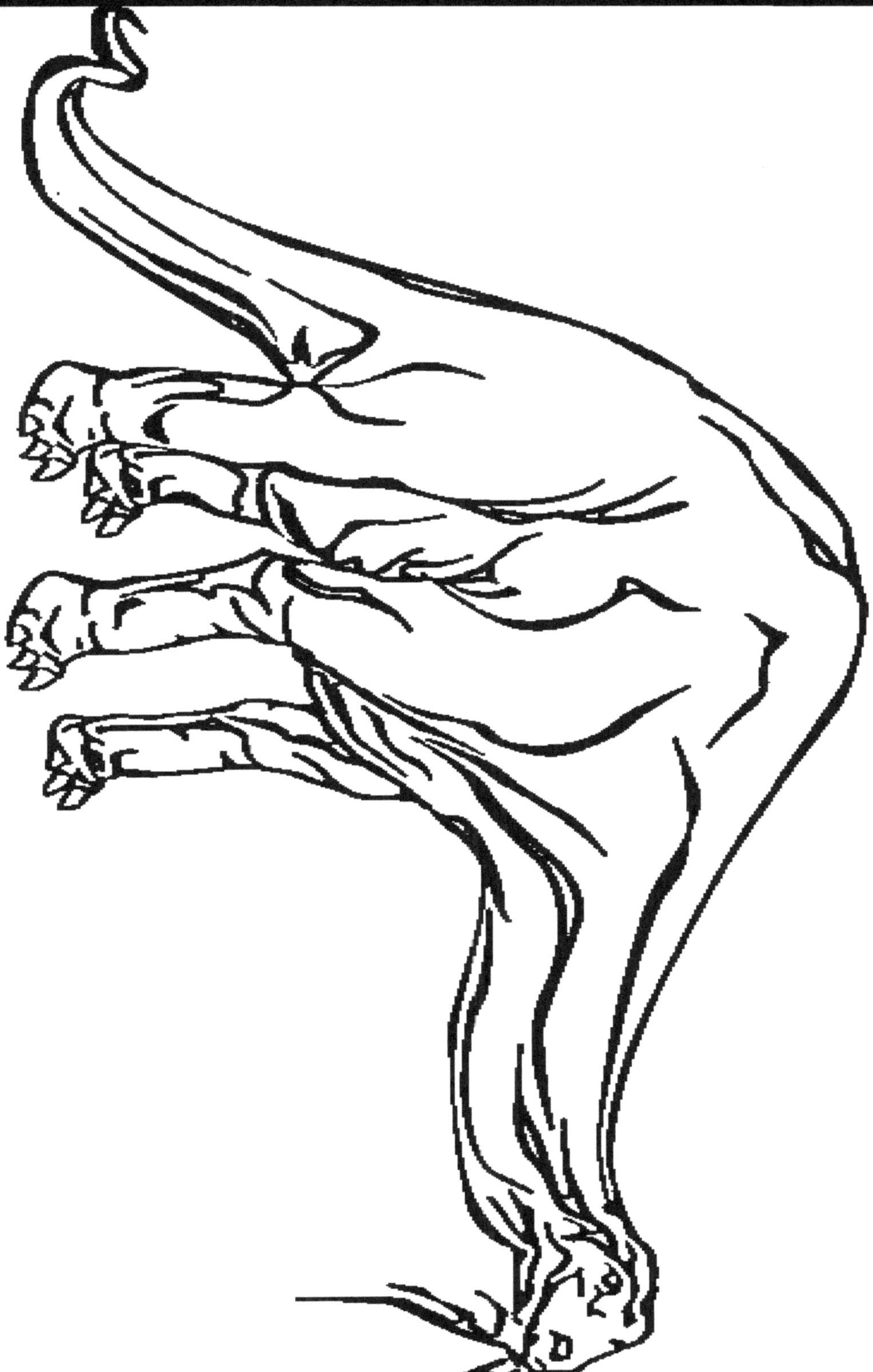

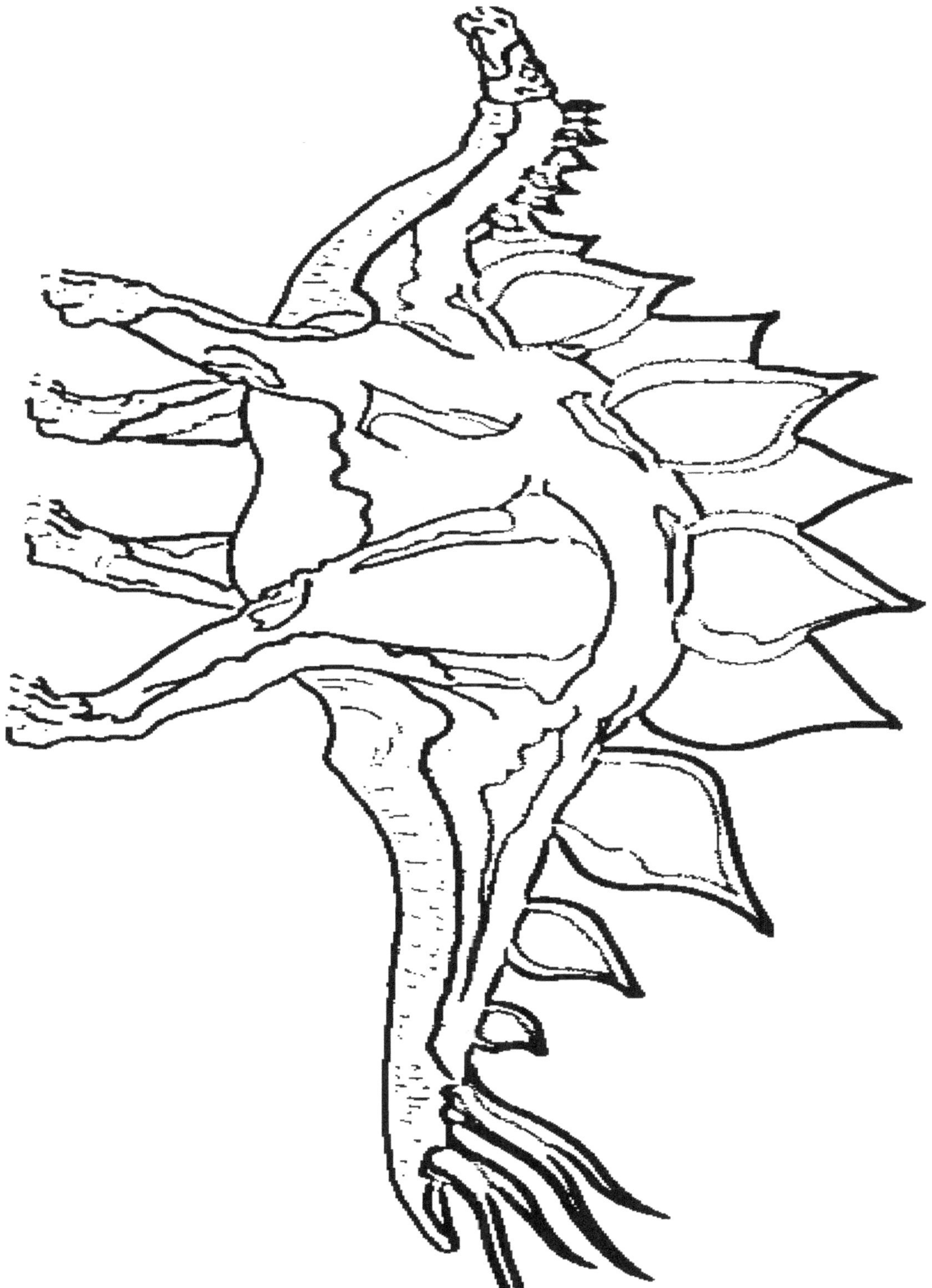

T-REX
ROAR
ROAR

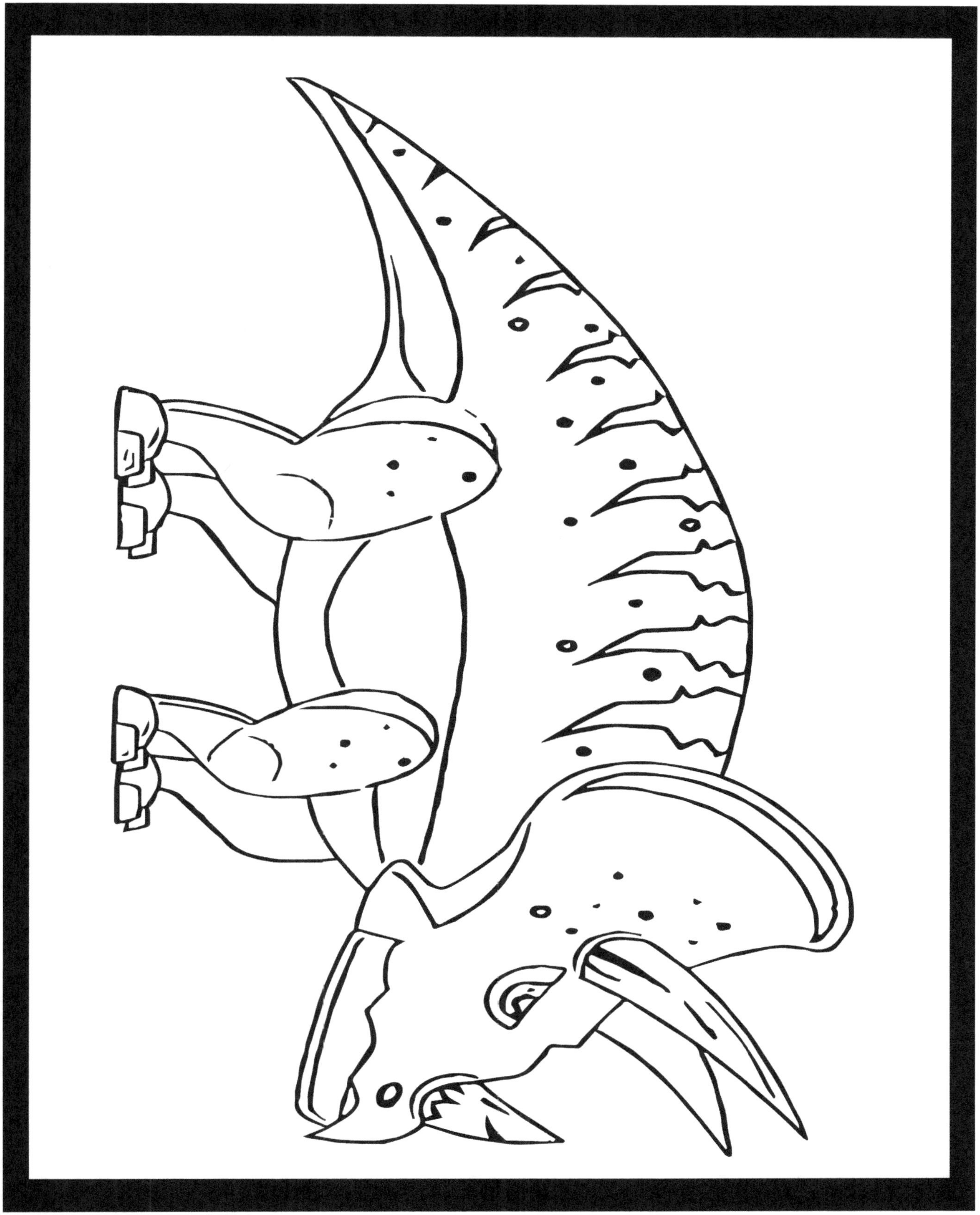

THE END

www.ingramcontent.com/pod-product-compliance
Lightning Source LLC
Chambersburg PA
CBHW080908220526
45466CB00011BA/3512
* 9 7 8 1 6 5 8 9 9 6 6 9 3 *